CHALLENGE YOUR IMAGINATION

Daniele Uleri

Copyright © 2020 - Daniele Uleri

All rights reserved.

Codice ISBN: 9798564499965

Thanks for buying this book!

I would like to know your opinion after using it.

I encourage you to write a review.

Your opinion is for me a contribution of great value.

Thank you for giving me some of your precious time.

Enjoy your Imagination!

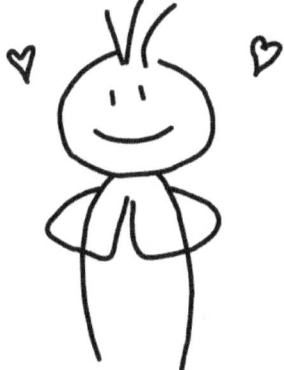

How to use it?

Each sheet contains a "start" figure from which to begin drawing.

Watch it carefully from every direction, pencil in hand, and free your imagination.

The page next to the "start" drawing has been deliberately left blank to give you more space in the development of your creation.

A simple drawing or a detailed one, it does not matter, just CREATE, and marvel at what you will be able to accomplish!

Clear the limits of your mind, outdo yourself, challenge friends, play with family.
You have a great tool on hand to keep your imagination active or to awaken it while HAVING FUN.

In the following pages you will find two practical examples that will give you an idea of how to use the "start" figures; each creation will be unique and personal.

Be a good observer and let your mind create the rest.

Imagination has no limits!

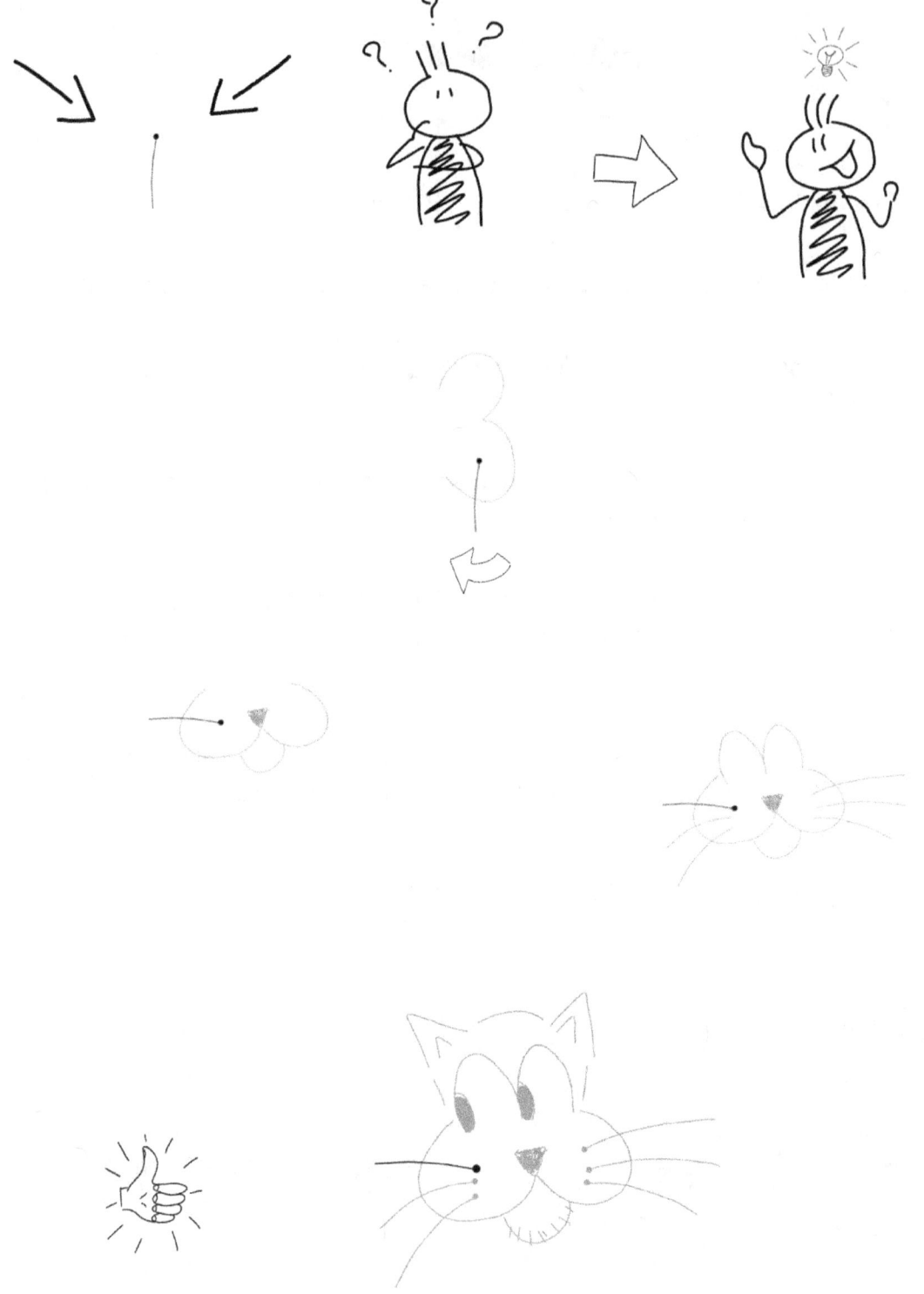

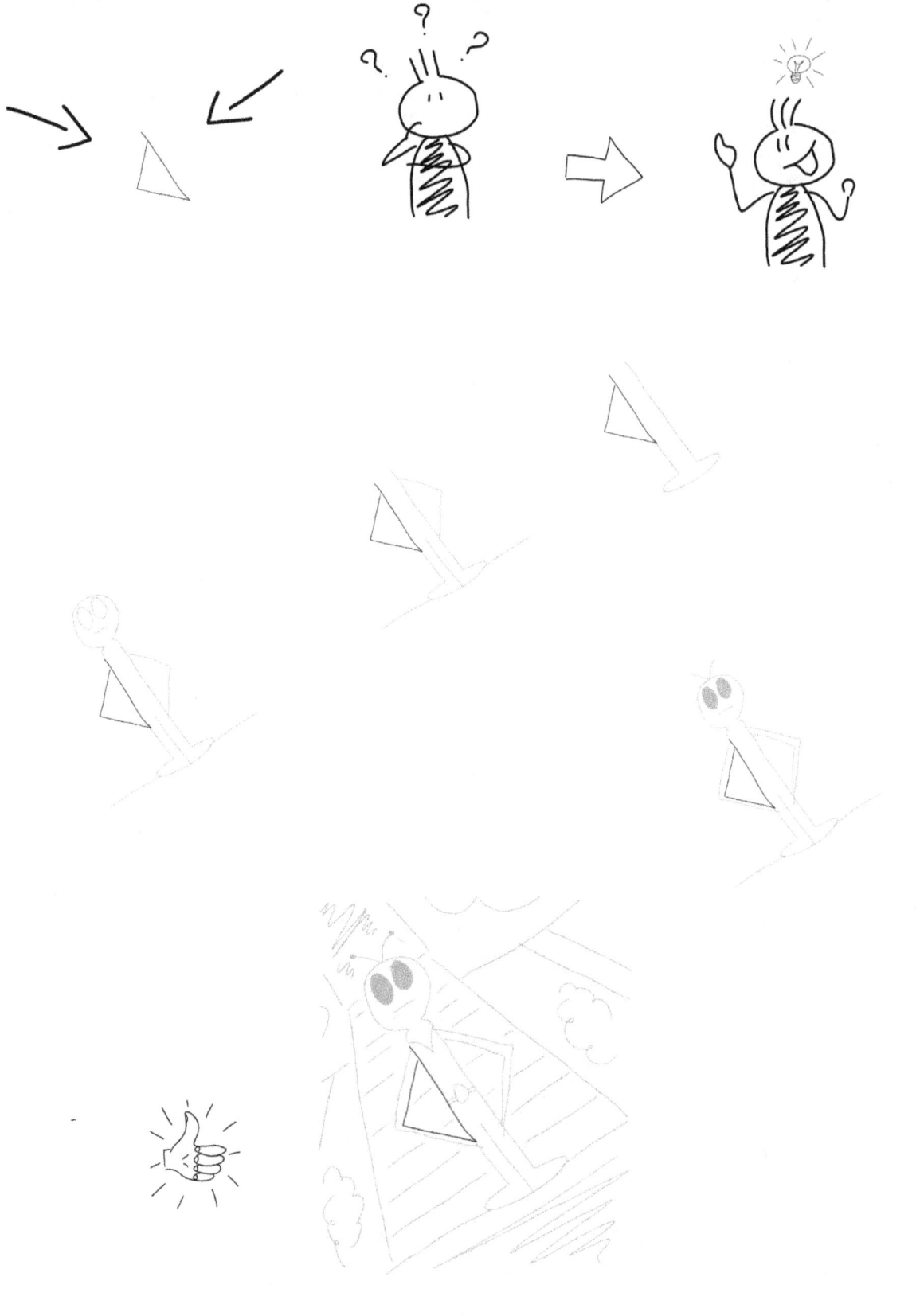

GOOD FUN

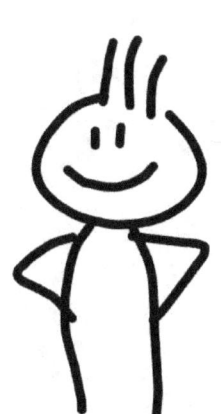

READY FOR THE CHALLENGE

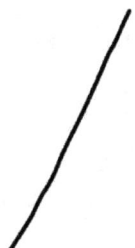

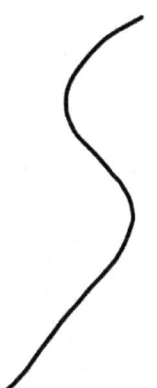

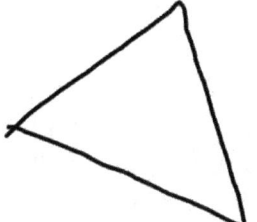

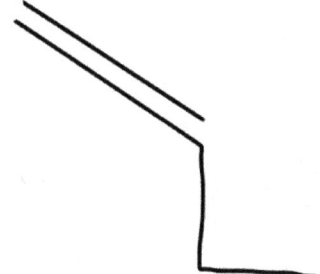

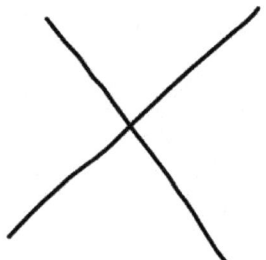

N

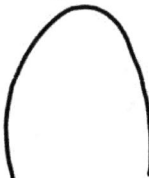

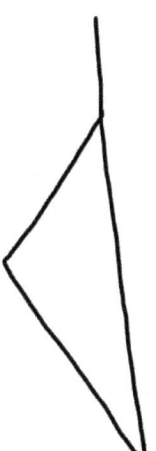

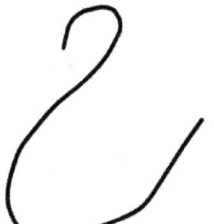

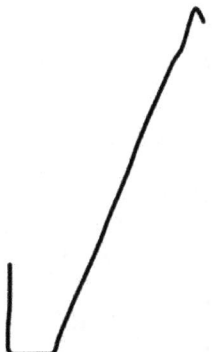

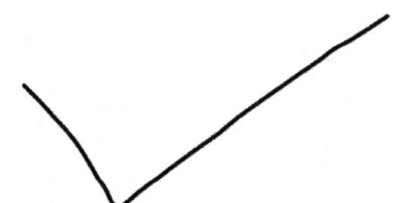

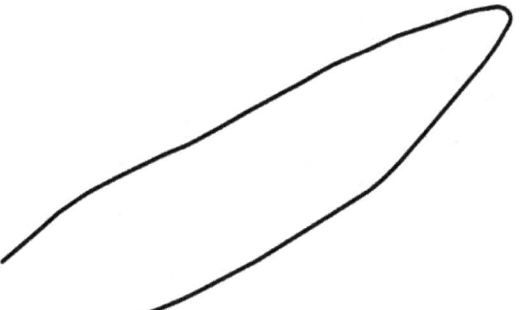

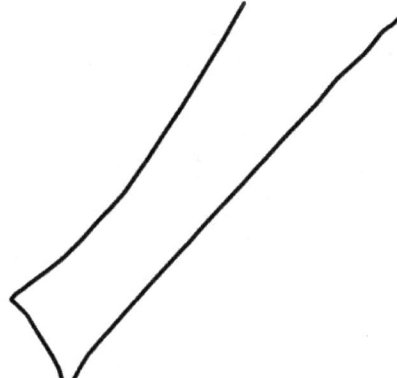

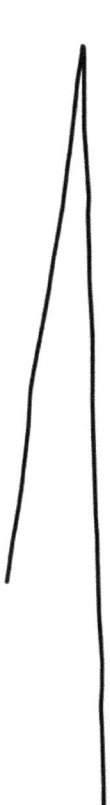

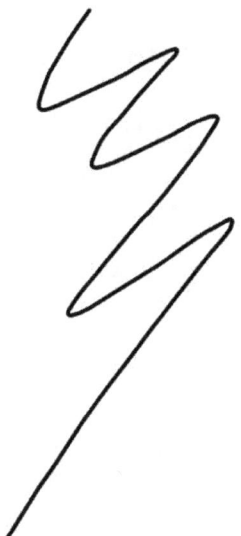

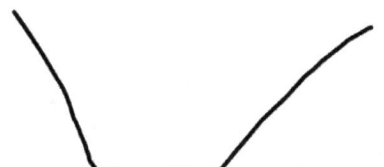

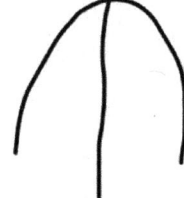

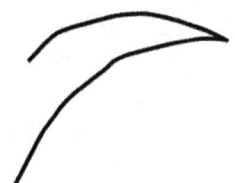

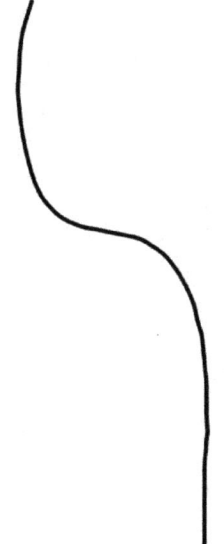

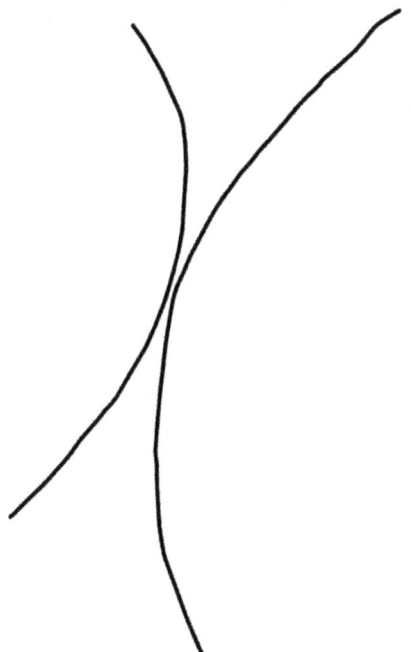

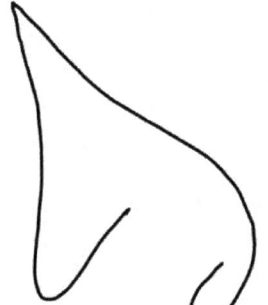

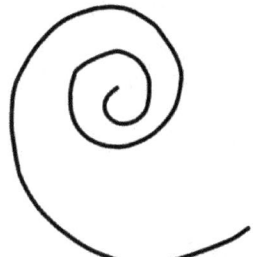

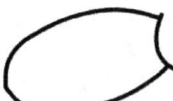

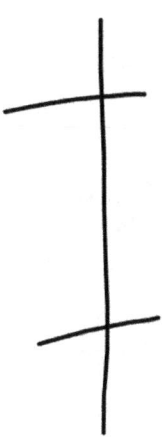

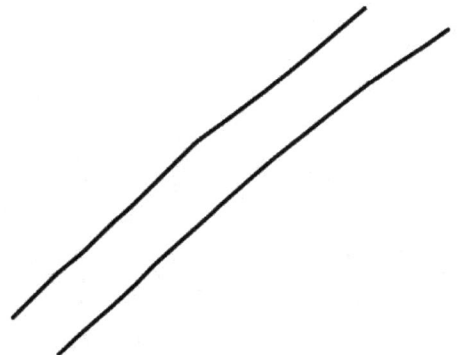

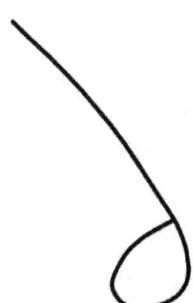

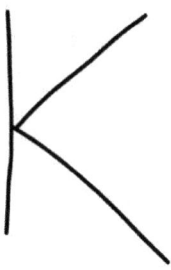

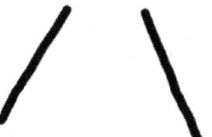

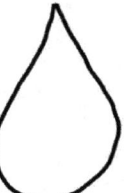

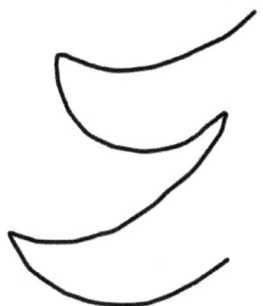

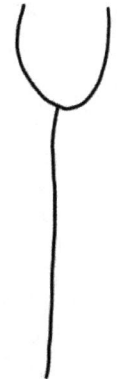

33

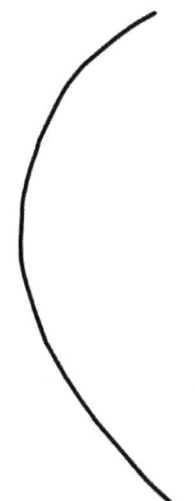

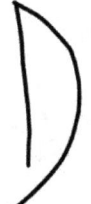

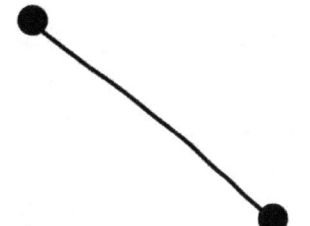

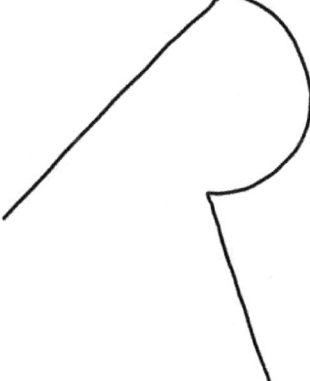

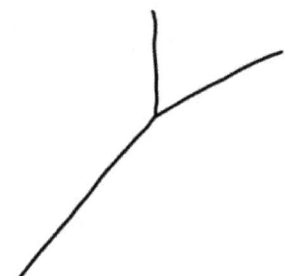

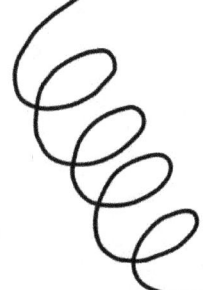

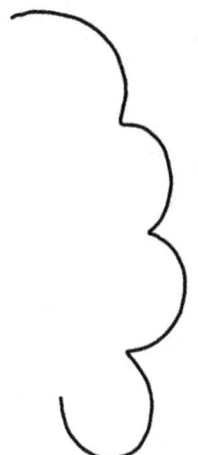

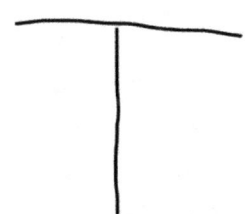

45

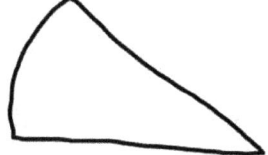

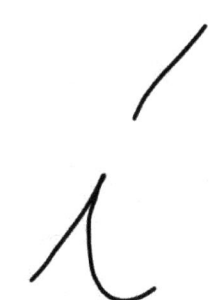

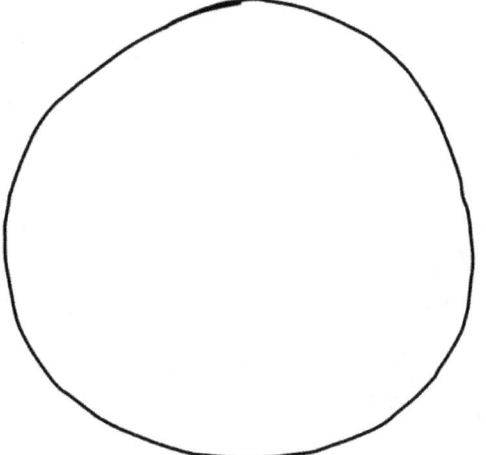

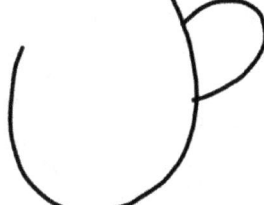

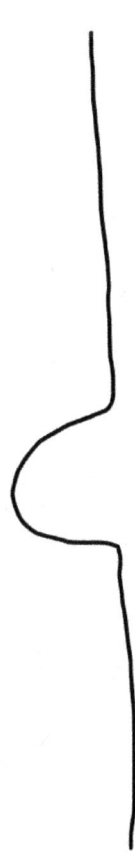

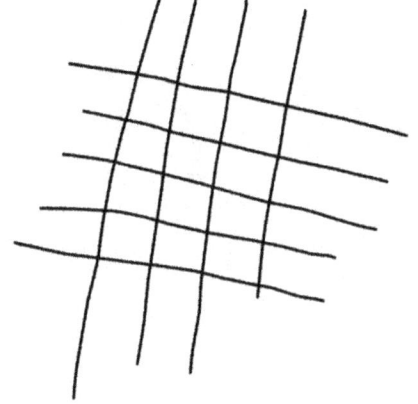

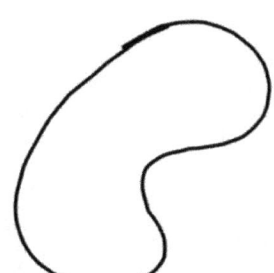

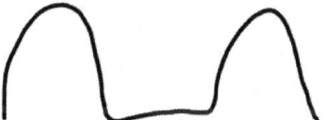

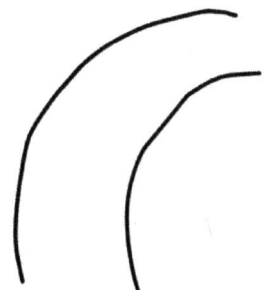

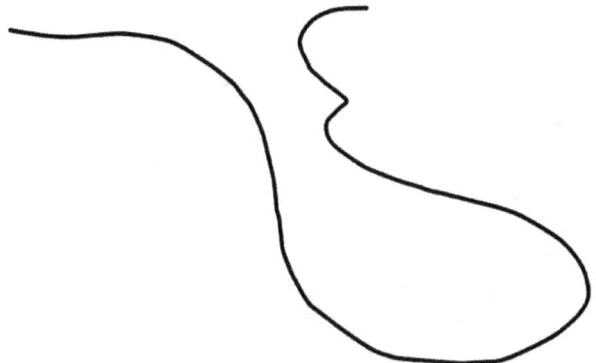

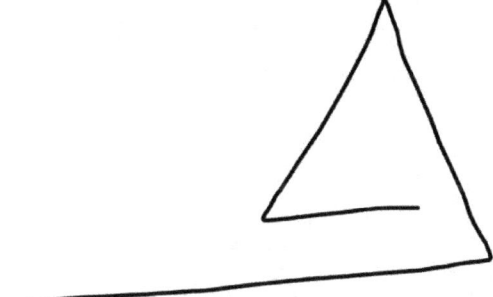

57

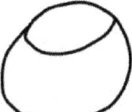

59

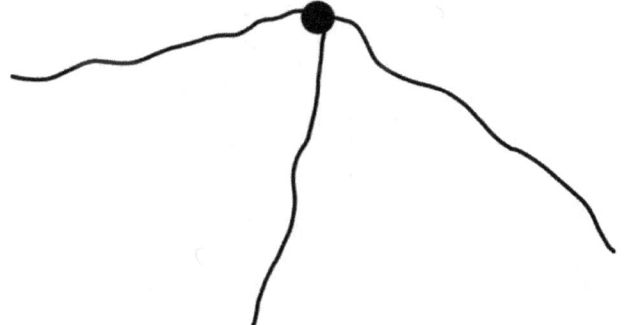

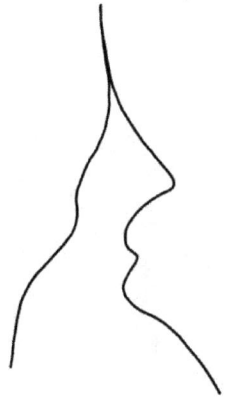

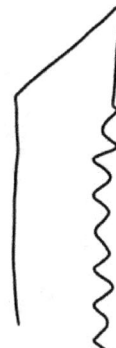

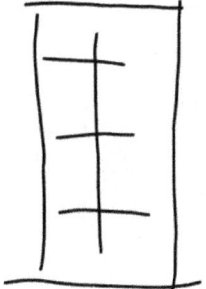

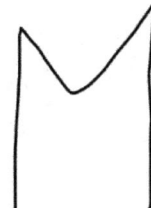

65

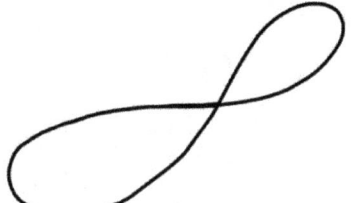

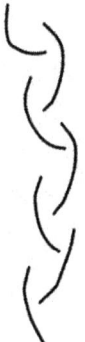

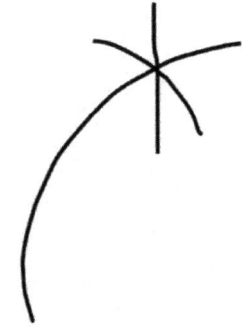

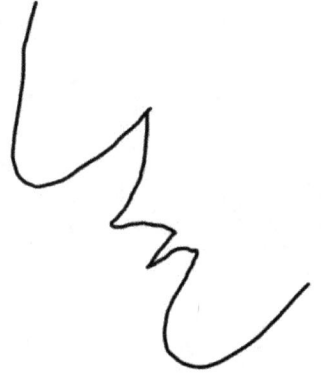

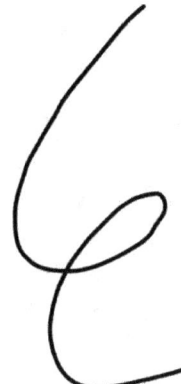

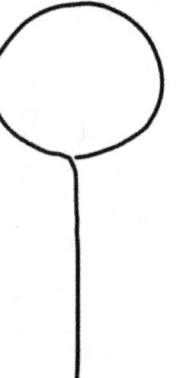

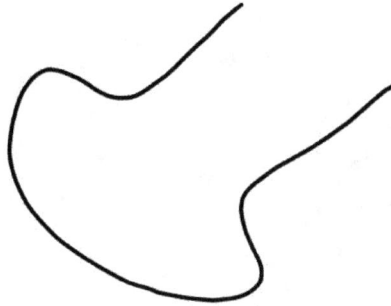

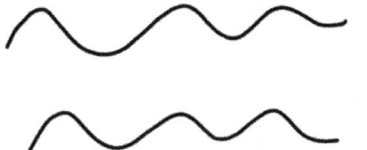

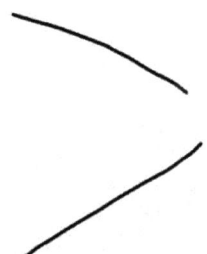

|||

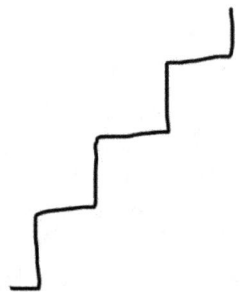

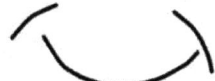

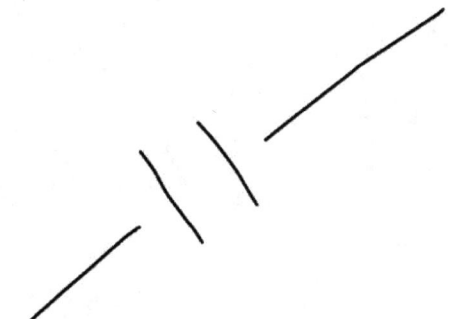

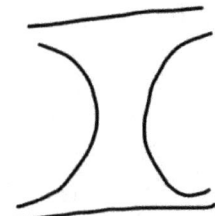

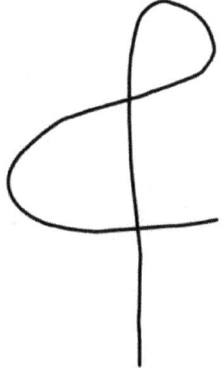

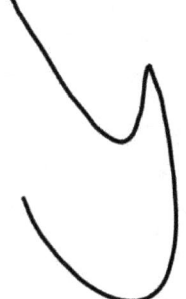

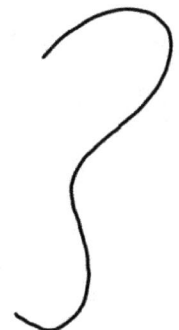

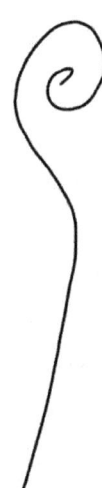

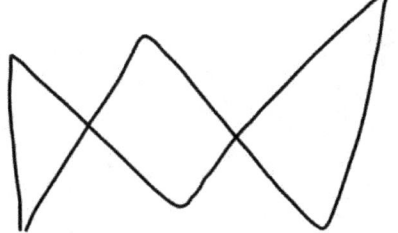

5

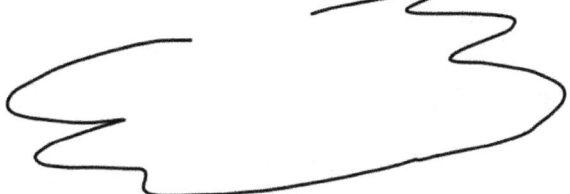

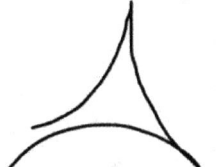

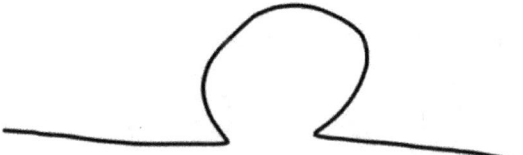

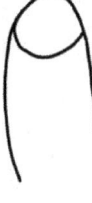

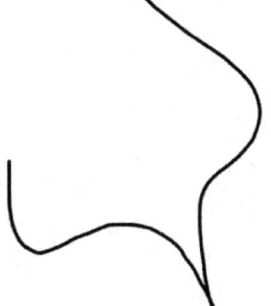

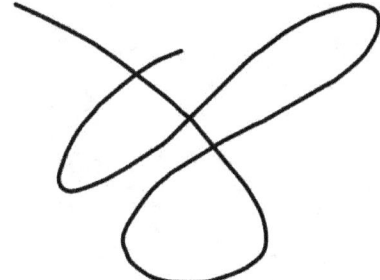

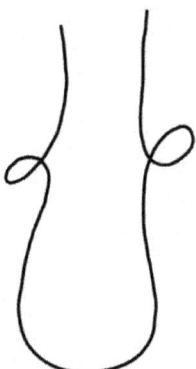

95

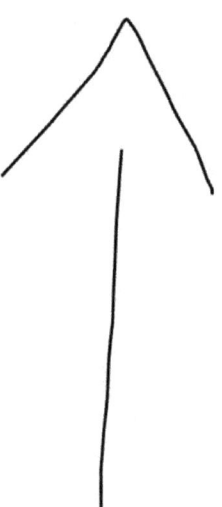

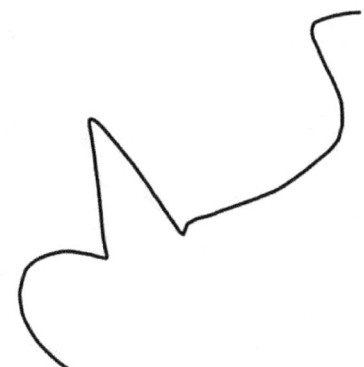

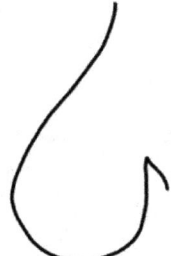

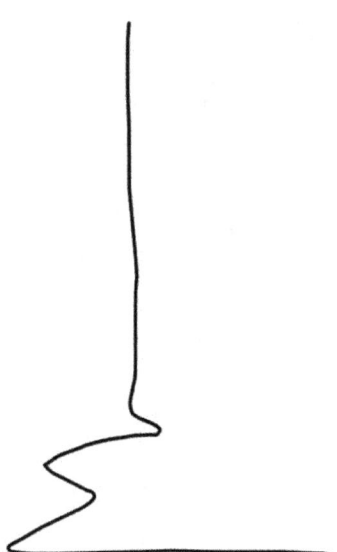

100

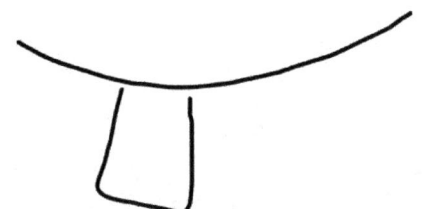

101

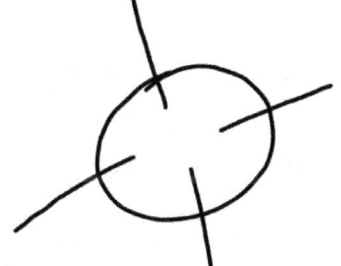

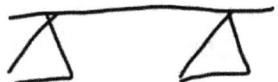

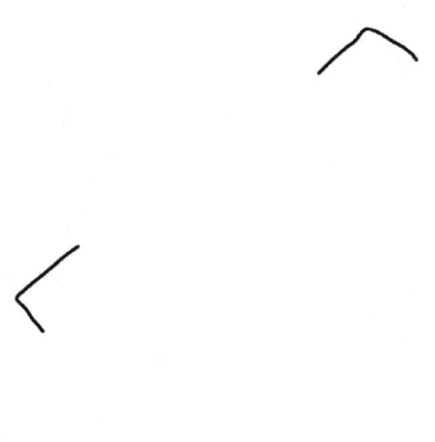

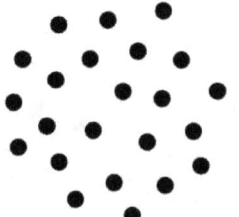

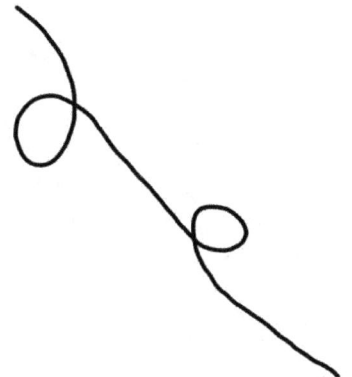

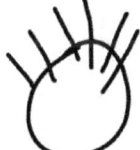

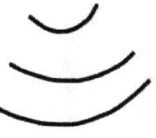

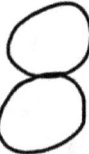

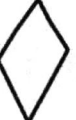

111

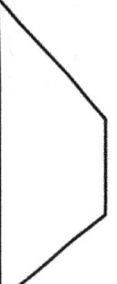

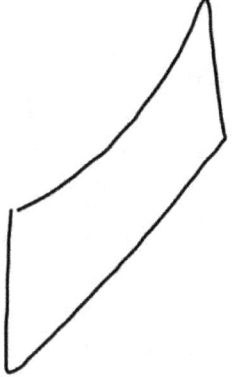

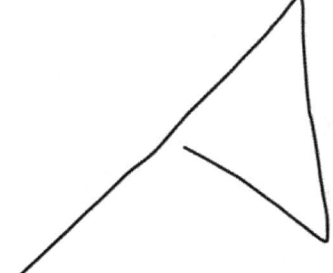

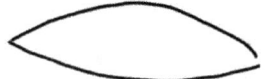

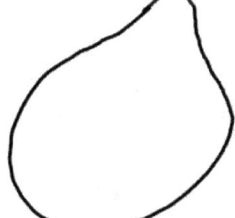

..

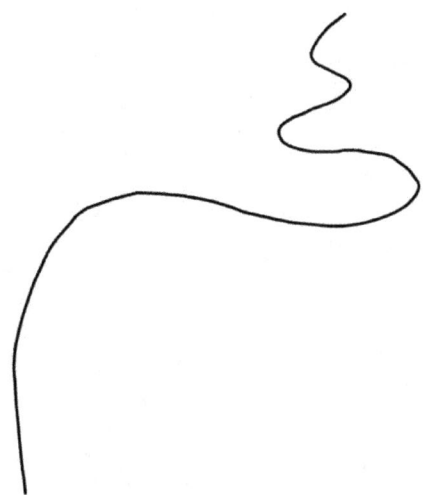

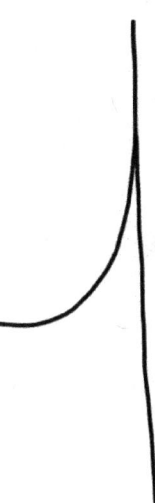

120

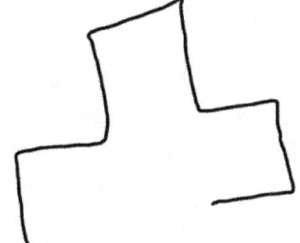

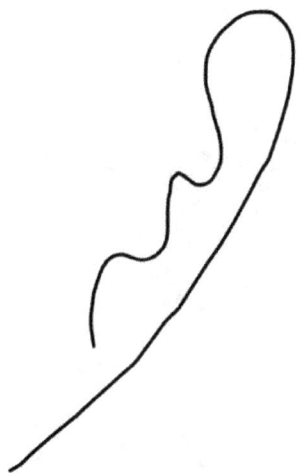

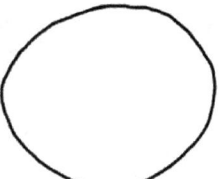

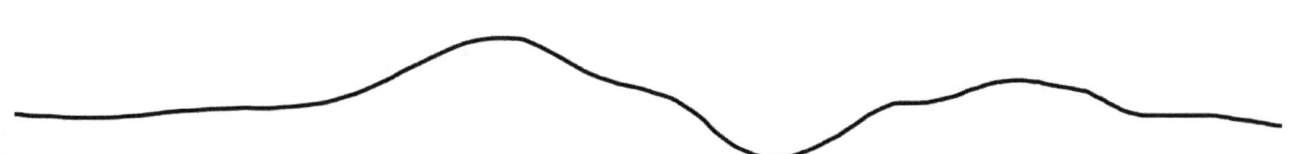

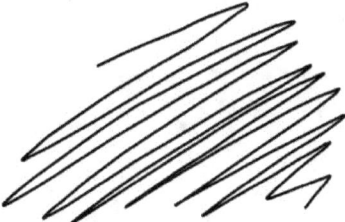

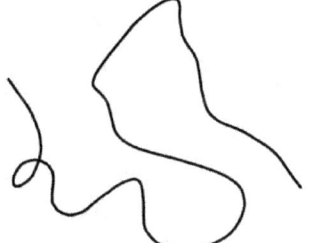

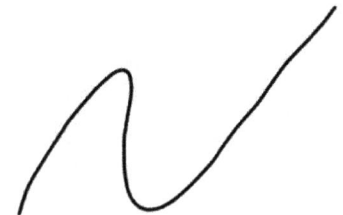

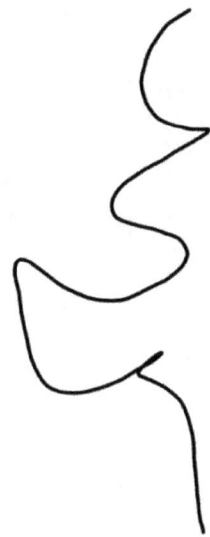

129

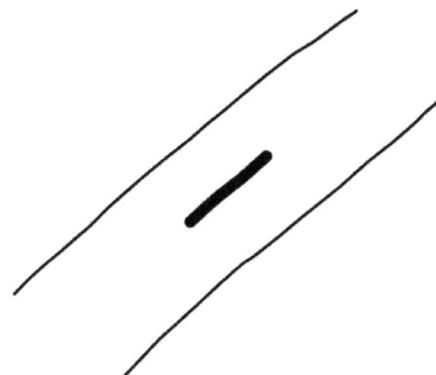

130

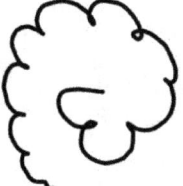

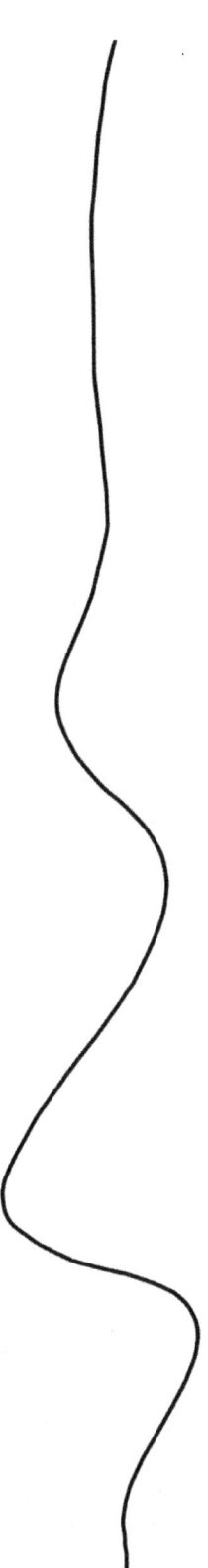

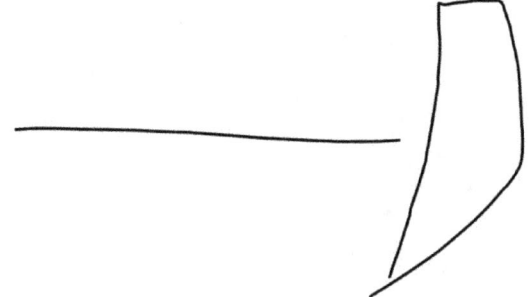

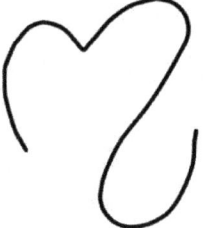

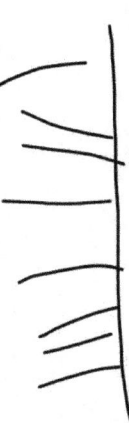

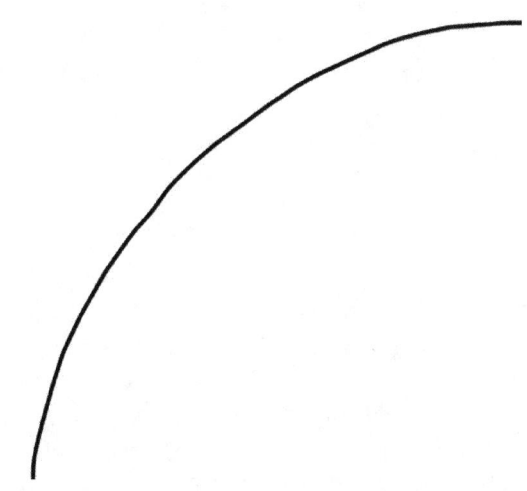

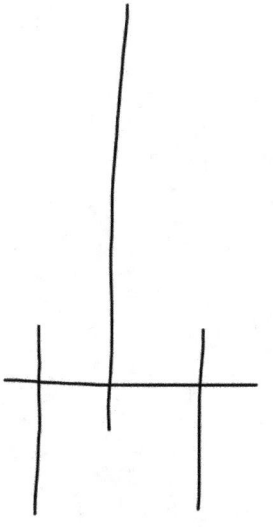

137

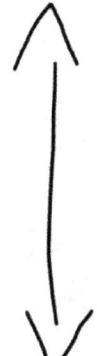

|—|—|—|—

139

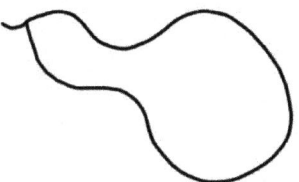

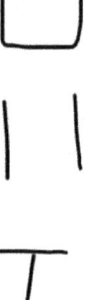

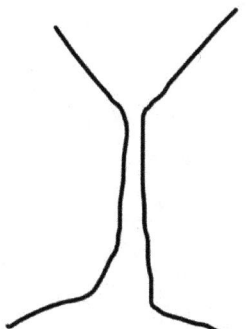

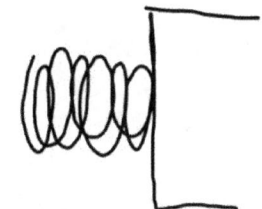

144

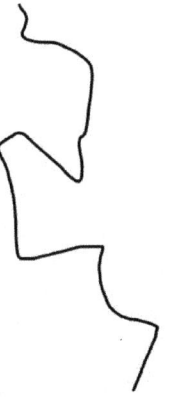

Thank you!
Thank you!
Thank you!

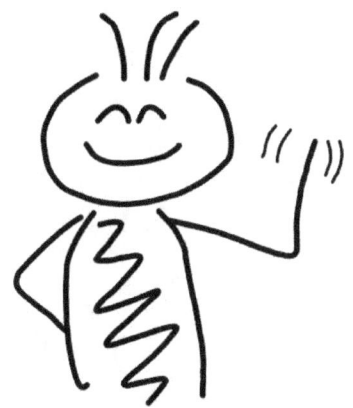

www.ingramcontent.com/pod-product-compliance
Lightning Source LLC
Chambersburg PA
CBHW081424220526
45466CB00008B/2262